I'm Reading About

CIVIL RIGHTS

GALLOPADE

by Carole Marsh

Printed and Manufactured in Peachtree City, GA., USA www.gallopade.com

Book design: Susan Van Denhende

Editor: Janice Baker

Photo Credits: Cover: www.marines.mil. Page 3: tharun15/Bigstock.com. Page 5A: Joeshmo/Bigstock.com; 5B: flippo/Bigstock.com. Pages 7, 9, 11, 15: Library of Congress. Page 13A: U.S. Air Force; 13B: Library of Congress. Page 17A: Library of Congress; 17B: Rediscovering-black-history.blogs.archives.gov. Page 18: Associated Press. Page 20: National Archives and Records Administration. Page 22: NASA. Page 24: www.mccall.com. Page 26: www.eji.org. Page 28A: U.S. Government Photo; 28B: National Archives and Records Administration; 28C: www.marines.mil. Page 30A: michaeljung/Bigstock.com; 30B: White House Press Office. Page 32A: National Archives and Records Administration; 32B: U.S. Department of State; 32C: White House Photo. Page 34: BackyardProductions/Bigstock.com.

The Civil Rights Movement was an important time in American history!

What was so important about the Civil Rights Movement?

Let's read about it and see!

CIVIL RIGHTS

What are civil rights?
Civil rights are basic rights that every person should have, like free speech and the right to vote.

Civil rights are for everyone: male and female, Black and white, young and old.

In the United States, civil rights are protected by the U.S. Constitution.

The Civil Rights Movement was a time when African Americans began to protest for equal rights.

Rights of the People

RIGHTS PROMISED

The story of the Civil Rights Movement
begins after the Civil War.

African Americans were freed from slavery!
The U.S. government passed laws
that promised them civil rights.

However, many people, especially people
in the Southern states,
did not want Black people to have their civil rights.
They passed laws that denied those rights!

Right to Vote

SEPARATION

Laws that separated Black people from white people were known as "Jim Crow laws."

Black people and white people were separated in public places like restaurants, hotels, schools, and bathrooms. They even had to use separate water fountains!

Other laws tried to keep Black people from voting. Some laws said they had to pay a tax to vote. Other laws forced them to pass a reading test to vote, but many Black people could not read!

Jim Crow Laws

CHANGES

In the early 1900s, some African Americans began to protest the unfair ways they were treated.

Some Black leaders formed a group called the NAACP to work for equal and fair treatment under the law.

Other Black leaders started schools. They knew education was a path to success in America!

NAACP stands for National Association for the Advancement of Colored People.

Education

Captain Smith on the
Jamestown; what the
Smiths plan
The Indians of Virginia

PROGRESS

In the mid 1900s, some African Americans broke long-standing barriers:

The Tuskegee Airmen in World War II were the first Black pilots to serve in the U.S. military. They helped create opportunities to serve in the armed forces!

Jackie Robinson was the first African American to play major league baseball. He opened the door for Black athletes in all sports!

Breaking Barriers

Tuskegee Airmen

Jackie Robinson

SCHOOLS

In the 1950s, a third-grader named Linda Brown made headlines in the Civil Rights Movement. Linda wanted to attend an all-white school near her house. The principal said no!

Linda's father went to court and won the case! The U.S. Supreme Court ruled that segregation in schools was not legal. After that, Black and white children could go to school together!

Segregation was the forced separation of Black and white people.

Schools Integrated

SCHOOLS

In Arkansas, nine Black students wanted
to attend an all–white high school.
The governor of the state said no,
but President Eisenhower said yes!

The students became known as the "Little Rock Nine."
They were very brave to take a stand.
Many people were very mean to the students.
Soldiers walked them into school to protect them!

Little Rock Nine

Rosa Parks

Another famous event in the Civil Rights Movement took place in Montgomery, Alabama. It happened on a city bus—where Black people and white people had to sit in different sections.

Rosa Parks was taking the bus home from work. She sat in the Black section, but the bus driver told her to give her seat to a white man. Rosa refused to give up her seat.

The police arrested Rosa and put her in jail!

Montgomery Bus Boycott

BOYCOTT

The incident with Rosa Parks started a movement!

Black citizens in Montgomery supported Rosa Parks.
They wanted to make their voices heard!
So, they refused to ride the city buses.
This became known as the "Montgomery Bus Boycott."

The bus boycott lasted for one year.
It cost the city of Montgomery a lot of money.
Finally, the U.S. Supreme Court ruled that segregation on public buses must end!

Martin Luther King, Jr.

LEADER

Martin Luther King, Jr. was a minister in Montgomery.
He became the leader of the Montgomery Bus Boycott.
Martin Luther King, Jr. called for nonviolent protests.
He did not want people to fight and get hurt.

The bus boycott sparked similar protests in other cities.
The Civil Rights Movement grew,
and Martin Luther King, Jr. became its leader!

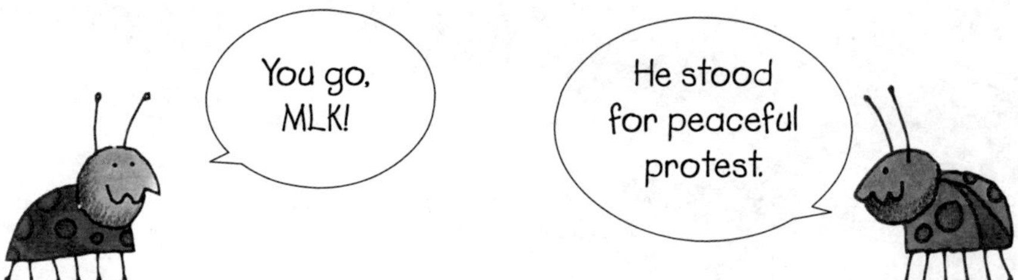

Sit-In Protest

SIT-INS

"Sit-ins" became another way for Black citizens to protest unfair treatment.

In North Carolina, four college students sat down at a whites-only lunch counter. They asked for coffee, but were not given any. They were asked to leave, but they refused.

Soon, other students held "sit-ins" across America! Angry people often insulted them and threw food at them. But the protesters never became violent.

Freedom Rides

FREEDOM RIDES

Another civil rights protest formed over segregation on buses that traveled from state to state.

Black and white Americans decided to ride together on buses from Washington, D.C. to the South. These trips were called "Freedom Rides."

Freedom Riders were often met by angry protesters. In Alabama, many of the first Freedom Riders were beaten and put in jail, and their bus was burned!

March on Washington

Martin Luther King, Jr. Speaks

Massive Crowd

Marchers with Signs

PEACE MARCH

In 1963, something really big happened!
More than 250,000 people headed to Washington, D.C.
They demanded equal rights for African Americans.
This event was called the "March on Washington."

Martin Luther King, Jr. made a famous speech.
He asked Americans to strive for a world where Black people and white people could live in peace.
The march made a huge impact on America!

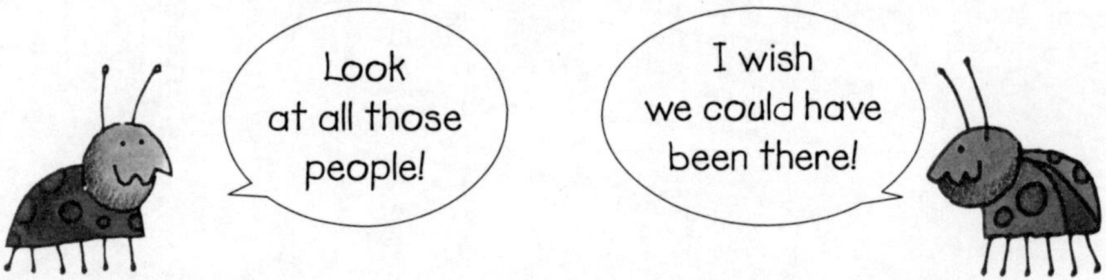

Laws Change America

President Johnson Signs 1964 Civil Rights Act

NEW LAWS

The March on Washington sent a clear message.
It told Congress: Vote YES on new civil rights laws!

Soon after, President Lyndon Johnson signed two laws:

- The Civil Rights Act: NO segregation and discrimination
- The Voting Rights Act: NO denying people's right to vote

The Civil Rights Act truly changed America!
It broke down the barriers that had held back
African Americans for 100 years!

African American Achievers

ACHIEVEMENTS

Those who fought for civil rights worked very hard and made many sacrifices. Because of the freedoms they won, many African Americans have achieved great things!

Here are just a few examples:

- Thurgood Marshall: First African American Supreme Court Justice
- Kamala Harris: First Female, African American, and Asian U.S. Vice President
- Barack Obama: First African American U.S. President

Martin Luther King, Jr. Memorial

LASTING LEGACY

The Civil Rights Movement changed America forever!

So that we never forget that struggle for equality, America has honored Martin Luther King, Jr. in many ways:

- A national holiday in January
- A national memorial in Washington, D.C.
- Streets, schools, and other places named for him across the U.S.

GLOSSARY

boycott: to refuse to buy, use, or participate in something as a protest

discrimination: unfair treatment of one person or group of people

integrate: to make something part of a larger unit; unite

legal: permitted by law

memorial: something preserving the memory of a person or event

nonviolent: not using physical force intended to hurt, damage, or kill

public place: place where all people can go

sacrifice: something you give up, usually for the sake of a better cause